Original title:
The Life You're Looking for Is Right Here

Copyright © 2025 Creative Arts Management OÜ
All rights reserved.

Author: Olivia Sterling
ISBN HARDBACK: 978-1-80566-113-9
ISBN PAPERBACK: 978-1-80566-408-6

Embrace the Now

Today's breakfast just might fly,
Waffle on the wall, oh my!
Syrup rivers flow with glee,
Pancakes dance, just wait and see.

Forget tomorrow, it's a hoot,
Yesterday's socks just won't suit.
Join the chaos, grab a snack,
Life's too short for plans, relax!

Horizon of Hidden Wonders

In my closet, a sock brigade,
One's a ninja, one's a maid.
Underneath the bed, oh dear,
Dust bunnies dance without fear.

The fridge hums songs of delight,
Leftovers planning a midnight bite.
Watch the curtains sway and bend,
You might find a ghostly friend!

Secrets Beneath the Surface

Underneath that bubbling stew,
A rubber duck quacks, 'Howdy-do?'
Pickles swim like little fish,
In lunchbox dreams, who knows the wish?

Beneath the couch, the remote hides,
Tug-o-war with candy resides.
Mystic crumbs from yesterday's feast,
Invite in ants for a weird feast!

Echoes of the Familiar

I hear the fridge, its ancient creak,
Like an old man who can't help speak.
"Leftovers, oh, do take a bite!"
Laughter echoes through the night.

The blender hums a secret tune,
In the dance-off with the moon.
A sock collection sings its song,
In this nonsense, I belong!

Unfolding in Time

Tick tock goes the clock, it's all a race,
Yet here I sit, with cake on my face.
Time's a trickster, pulling my nose,
But laughter's the prize, as everyone knows.

What's on tomorrow? I don't even care,
Yesterday's socks? Why are they a pair?
Each moment's a gift, wrapped up in delight,
With confetti for breakfast and joy in the night.

Adventures in Your Backyard

Grab your sun hat, it's time for a stroll,
The squirrels are plotting, that's their goal!
A bike made of sticks and a flag made of cheese,
In my backyard kingdom, I reign with such ease.

Jumping on trampolines made out of grass,
A castle of cushions where no one can pass.
My friends are the bugs, and my snacks are the leaves,
Who needs far away lands? This is where magic weaves!

As You Breathe, So You Live

Inhale the giggles, exhale the frowns,
I'm juggling my dreams while wearing new crowns.
Each breath is a party, a wild, silly dance,
Where funny hats twirl, and who knows my chance?

When life gives you lemons, I'd rather make pie,
With a twisty straw hat and a wink in my eye.
Breathe in the silly, let out all the sighs,
You might find confetti where boredom just lies.

Signs of Abundance

Look at this sandwich, it's tall as can be,
With pickles and chips, smiling back at me.
Abundance is knowing that joy fills your plate,
Even when it's just cereal, don't underestimate!

The clouds are fluffy like cotton candy dreams,
Sunshine is free, or so it seems.
With bubbles and giggles all soaring above,
There's plenty of fun, there's plenty of love.

Serendipity in Stillness

A sock on a chair, what a sight!
It surely must be lost in flight.
Coffee spills like art on my shirt,
Yet here I sit, not feeling hurt.

Birds audition for my laugh today,
Singing tunes in a quirky display.
Can a cat really catch its own tail?
Life's surprises, a comical trail.

The Canvas of Ordinary Days

A spoon flies out of the drawer,
It dreams of flight, yet drops and bore.
The toast burns with a fierce delight,
It's charred perfection, what a sight!

In my garden, weeds take the throne,
Claiming victory, like kings they've grown.
Yet daisies peek through with a grin,
Even chaos can have a spin.

Heartbeats in the Quiet

A hiccup breaks the silent gloom,
Just me and my imagination's room.
The cat and I share a whispered plight,
As she ponders if she's a lion tonight.

The fridge hums a familiar tune,
Like it knows an old friend will be home soon.
The clock chuckles, tick-tock in jest,
Reminding me that time's quite a guest.

Unseen Joys of the Mundane

I dance with my mop to no one near,
While singing songs only I can hear.
The plant waves as if it can tell,
That life is perfect, oh so swell!

Stairs creak in a playful song,
Each step a note, where I belong.
A sock puppet whispers, 'Take it slow!'
In this silly world, I'm the star of the show.

Pages of the Present

In pajamas, I sit with glee,
Coffee spills, oh, dear me!
Today's too bright to sit and fuss,
Let's trade our plans for just a bus.

Flip the pages, what's next, my friend?
A dance with the cat, on that we depend!
Adventures call, don't check the weather,
Life's a joke, let's laugh together.

Moments That Matter

A sock on the floor, oh what a sight,
It sparkles so boldly in morning light.
Let's cherish each tumble, each joyful slip,
For laughter's the true shaping of our trip.

Counting the crumbs, the snacks we munch,
In this silly bubble, let's have a hunch:
What's better than pizza and a side of pie?
Moments like these make time fly by!

Anchored in Today

My to-do list looks like a monster's feast,
But back there's a donut that whispers, "At least!"
With every bite, I'm sailing away,
To shores of delight, where I wish to stay.

There's magic in socks that don't quite match,
Like finding a pen with a funky scratch.
Right now is a riddle, a goofy charade,
With giggles and smiles, let's not be afraid.

A Kaleidoscope of Now

Twirl around, catch your breath,
Life's a mischief, it's no death.
Kaleidoscope dreams spin in my head,
With marshmallow clouds and chocolate spread.

Let's paint our thoughts with crayons bright,
And dance with shadows in the soft moonlight.
The wild art of moments, oh what a show,
Grab a friend and let your worries go!

Currents of Continuity

Lost socks in the dryer, it's a tale we know,
They dance and they twirl, putting on a show.
Fridge humming softly, a symphony of snacks,
Life's little treasures hiding in the cracks.

Chairs that creak like old men in jest,
They speak of a comfort, a lingering rest.
Dog rolls in mud, like it's a spa day,
While cats plot their reign, in a most regal way.

Harmony in Happenstance

Spill coffee on the shirt, it's a fashion parade,
We call it art now, a bold charade.
Umbrellas flipped inside out in the rain,
Who knew chaos could have such a gain?

Lost on a stroll, but found a good pie,
Street performing pigeons, oh my, oh my!
Every little hiccup, a reason to grin,
Life's hilarious rhythm, where can we begin?

Epiphanies in the Commonplace

Mismatched sneakers on the run, what a sight,
Every step is a giggle, pure delight.
Banana peels lurking, oh what a tease,
Timing a trip, with such graceful ease.

Mailboxes whisper forgotten dreams,
While squirrels hold meetings, or so it seems.
In the chaos of crumbs, we find the divine,
Wonders in mundane, like jam on a vine.

Portraits of the Present

Neighbors yelling from across the street,
Who knew storytelling could be so sweet?
Remote controlled chaos during TV night,
Each button a mystery, oh what a fright!

Butterfingers drop snacks with a clatter,
Creating a moment where giggles splatter.
Life's silly snapshots, painted so bright,
In the gallery of now, everything's right.

Dance of the Unremarkable

In pajamas all day, I groove so stiff,
The fridge is my stage, for a midnight lift.
Who needs a crowd when chips are my cheers?
I dance with the dust bunnies, laughter and beers.

The vacuum is loud, but I feel like a star,
Twisting and turning, I'm the best by far.
Not a soul sees my moves, but oh, what a sight!
I'm waltzing with whimsy, in my living room light.

Threads of the Here and Now.

In a world full of socks, mismatched and bold,
I knit a fine tale, with stories untold.
My cat's the critic, with a paw on my work,
He judges my choices with a flick and a smirk.

Coffee in hand, I measure my joy,
On this tangled up thread, I play like a toy.
A splash of spilled dreams, a pinch of good cheer,
This present's a puzzle, stitched up, never clear.

A Treasure Found Within

In the depths of my couch, I find hidden gold,
Forgotten old snacks and stories retold.
Change jingles softly, like secrets they keep,
Nestled in cushions, where memories sleep.

A treasure map drawn with crumbs as my guide,
Each nibble I munch feels like a fun ride.
I sell my findings to the quirky cat crew,
Who trade me their whiskers for a taste of my stew.

Paths Unseen

In the garden of chaos, I wander with glee,
Finding lost socks and a missing car key.
Each twist and each turn, I giggle and run,
Cracking the code of a day full of fun.

Bumps in the road bring laughter and groans,
Worms as my buddies, discussing their homes.
With maps made of crumpled-up takeout receipts,
I travel through life on wobbly feet.

The Heart's Compass

In a world full of maps, I lost my way,
But my heart chirps louder, come what may.
With a compass of snacks, I'll surely thrive,
Finding joy in crumbs, feeling so alive.

I asked a squirrel for directions one day,
He just laughed and ran off to play.
The signposts are gibberish, but that's just fine,
I'll dance with the shadows, let my spirit shine.

Now, Not Tomorrow

Why wait for tomorrow, when today's so bright?
I'll wear polka dots and toss confetti light.
With socks that don't match and a smile so wide,
I'll chase after rainbows on a goofball ride.

The to-do list can wait; it's partly to blame,
For all of the fun that's stuck in a frame.
So grab your weird hat, let's serenade the noon,
With laughter that echoes like a happy tune.

Embrace the Ordinary

In the ordinary moments, magic appears,
Like finding lost socks or dodging small fears.
I'll stir my coffee and turn the day round,
When I spill it a little, I giggle, I'm found.

Why chase after grandeur, when joy is in cream,
Or the spark of a joke, a silly old dream?
With quips and some bubbles, let's toast to the mundane,
Stirring laughs in our cups, let's dance in the rain.

A Canvas of Possibilities

With brushes of fate, I'll splash bright hues,
In a canvas that giggles, with whimsical views.
I'll paint with bananas and a twirl of zest,
Creating a masterpiece, an artful jest.

As the splatters now mingle, I see what could be,
A duck in a top hat, a cat sipping tea.
So let's color outside the lines of our plans,
With laughter as our palette, we'll make silly scans.

Pathways of the Present

Stumbling on my morning jog,
Chasing down a hefty fog,
My sneakers squeak like rubber ducks,
Oh, the joy of silly luck!

A wayward cat, a coffee spill,
Life's absurd, it gives a thrill,
I trip on dreams too bright to see,
And laughter's there to set me free!

Bicycle bells and goofy cheers,
We laugh away our silly fears,
A squirrel chases my fallen crumbs,
He knows the fun that always comes!

With every twist and every turn,
In each face, a lesson learned,
The present's quirks, a playground grand,
Just dance along, don't make a plan!

Blossoms in the Sidestreets

In sidestreets where the daisies bloom,
I trip over my own costume,
A hat too big, two left-foot shoes,
I'm quite the sight, yet can't refuse!

Pigeons squawk and steal my fries,
They strut around with lofty pride,
A dog in shades goes for a stroll,
While I just laugh and lose control!

A ladybug with fancy wings,
Dances like she knows all things,
I tumble down the very lane,
Where joy is found in silly pain!

Life tumbles on with goofy grace,
A merry dance, a funny race,
Embrace the quirks, it's not a test,
In sidestreets, we simply jest!

Tides of Here and Now

Riding waves of ice cream bliss,
A cone in one hand, oh how I miss,
A seagull swoops, a theft so grand,
My treat's no longer in my hand!

The beach towel's flipped, it takes a dive,
I wonder if it'll still survive,
Flip-flops thrown with giddy grace,
A treasure hunt in sunny space!

Sandcastles rise, but tides don't care,
Each wave's a joke, a playful dare,
We laugh as moats begin to fade,
Ocean's humor on parade!

In every splash, a giggle's found,
Laughter echoes all around,
With salty hair and joyful sighs,
Let's soak in life, oh how time flies!

The Art of Being

Painting days with colors bright,
I draw a mustache on the night,
A little cat with polka dots,
Artistic blunders? Oh, who's got?

Juggling thoughts like oranges tossed,
In this circus, I'm the boss,
Every flop, a masterpiece,
Life's gallery never sees a cease!

Dancing shadows on the wall,
Mimic moves, we laugh and fall,
A canvas spills with coffee stains,
Artistry revealed in silly gains!

So here we are, just you and me,
Masterpieces made of glee,
In every scribble, laughter sings,
This is the joy that living brings!

The Journey Begins Here

Pack your bags, leave the stress,
A suitcase full of silliness,
The road is calling, come take a ride,
With laughter as our trusty guide.

Jump in the car, sing off-key,
Dancing in our seats, feeling free,
Every bump will shake our cares,
As we chase the wind, forget our layers.

Stop for ice cream, two scoops each,
With sprinkles to inspire our speech,
This detour is a map to joy,
More fun than any fancy toy!

Look around, the world's a stage,
You're the star, flip a new page,
The journey's all that we declare,
Smiles await us, everywhere!

Heartbeats of the Present

Tick-tock, the clock's gone mad,
Spilling thoughts of good and bad,
But here's a secret, lean in close,
  Every tick's a chance to boast.

Dance like no one's watching you,
Trip on shoes that are two sizes too,
The present's got the moves we crave,
And a giggle's what we always save.

Hold a spatula, flip a pancake,
Add some syrup, make a mistake,
Life's a recipe, messy and great,
Taste the sweetness while it waits!

Live like jelly, wobble around,
With silly faces, we'll astound,
Every heartbeat's bold and bright,
In the now, we take our flight!

Wonders in the Everyday

Coffee spills, it's quite a sight,
Looks like art in morning light,
A sprinkle of chaos, a dash of cream,
Everyday magic, like a dream.

Lost my keys, but found a cat,
He's lounging there, imagine that!
With whiskers twitching, oh so grand,
In the simple, wonders expand.

Missed the bus, it's no big deal,
I'll take a stroll, maybe steal a meal,
A bakery whiff calls me near,
That's a treat to lift the cheer!

Life's a circus, run with the thrill,
Catch the giggles, it's quite the skill,
Every moment, a playful jest,
In the now, we find our best!

Beyond What We Seek

Chasing dreams down every street,
But wait, look there, a dancing beat,
A squirrel in shades is leading the way,
Who knew this would make our day?

Chase the clouds, give them a tickle,
Let's laugh until our bellies wiggle,
What we seek is just a frame,
Sometimes quirky is the aim.

Puddle jumps and rainy days,
Splashing color in all the grays,
In muddy boots and laughter's cheer,
Life's a canvas, bright and clear!

Forget the map, let's make our own,
Adventure sprouts where seeds are sown,
In what we find, we finally see,
That joy was waiting, endlessly!

Songs of the Season

In winter, I can't find my glove,
But the snowman sings and dances above.
My hot chocolate's cold, is that a crime?
At least the marshmallows float just fine.

Spring blossoms sprout in a flash,
Yet my allergies hit with a loud crash.
I sneeze a tune, oh what a show,
The bees hum back, a vibrant flow.

Summer brings heat, the sun's on a spree,
I'm grilling burgers, but they're all charred, you see!
The fireflies blink, my favorite guests,
They light up the night, and they do their best.

Autumn leaves fall, a dance in the breeze,
I trip on a pumpkin; oh, sweet, sweet tease!
Cider in hand, I grin wide and bright,
Who knew a mishap could end up just right?

Grounded in Gratitude

Woke up today, without a single sock,
Thankful my toaster pops toast, not a rock.
My cat frowns at me, what have I done?
But her purring means I'm still number one.

Cereal spills all over the floor,
But who needs neat? My heart wants more.
Each crunch a blessing, each splash a cheer,
Thankful for chaos that comes every year.

The neighbor's dog took my favorite shoe,
Yet in my garden, daisies bloom anew.
I laugh as I chase it, it feels so right,
Grateful for mischief that brings sheer delight.

Rain on the window, it beats a drum,
While I find joy in the hum of some.
Umbrellas flip inside out like a dance,
Thankful for life and its silly chance.

A Map of Moments

I lost my keys in the fridge, oh dear,
A map reveals adventures not so clear.
Each corner I turn, gets wilder still,
My GPS laughs; it's testing my will.

The coffee stains mark where I've been,
They tell stories of victories, woe, and sin.
I draw a line from mishap to cheer,
This messy route makes everything clear.

In every stumble, there's a dance and a flip,
Mapping my life, each joy a trip.
I write it all down with crayons and zest,
A rainbow's worth living, I count as the best.

So follow your heart through the twists and bends,
The map is a journey that never ends.
No treasure chest buried, just laughter and play,
This cartographer's joy is in every day.

Serendipity Underfoot

Walking on sidewalks, I trip over fate,
A squirrel steals my sandwich; is that really a date?
Chasing down breadcrumbs, I can't help but laugh,
Nature's a prankster, a quirky craft.

In puddles I splash in the rain-soaked delight,
My umbrella flips, it's a comical sight.
I dance with the raindrops, they twirl and they spin,
Each drop is a tickle, let the fun begin!

Every corner I turn leads to silly surprise,
A strange man in a hat with big googly eyes.
He winks as he juggles, oh what a show,
Life's odd little moments steal the main flow.

So here's to the giggles that bubble up high,
With laughter beneath me, I'll soar and I'll fly.
Serendipity waits with each step that I take,
Life's merry mischief, oh, the joy it can make!

Illumination in the Everyday

In the morning light we brew,
Coffee smiles and waves hello.
Toast pops up, it's quite a scene,
Butter sliding, golden sheen.

Socks mismatched on the floor,
Laughing at the daily chore.
The cat steals the seat I claimed,
Playful antics never tamed.

Rainy days can't dampen cheer,
Puddles splash, we disappear.
Umbrellas twirl like dance of glee,
Life's a party, can't you see?

So here's to the quirky grind,
Finding joy in what we find.
In the chaos, love is clear,
Every moment, worth a cheer!

Radiance of Routine

Toothpaste battles every morn,
Fighting foes, I feel reborn.
Socks become my fashion plight,
Wearing stripes with all my might.

Lunch breaks come, a food dispute,
Trading snacks, oh what a hoot!
Sandwiches with tales they tell,
Of office chaos, oh so swell.

Evening comes, the couch is king,
Remote fights for the final fling.
Shows collide like stars at night,
Bingeing on laughter feels just right.

As I settle in my nest,
Life's a comedy at its best.
Routine shines with silly joy,
It's the little things we enjoy!

Beyond the Veil of Tomorrow

Plans and dreams float on a cloud,
But today's the stage, let's be loud.
Forget the stress of what's to come,
Turn it up, let's sing and hum.

Tomorrow's worries can just wait,
Let's celebrate and not be late.
Jokes exchanged like secret maps,
Laughter echoes, what a clap!

In the chaos of the now,
We'll dance and laugh, I take a bow.
Every mishap, a comic gem,
Life's a show, and we're the stem.

So join the fun, the time is bright,
We're the stars that light the night.
In each second, magic flows,
Turn the mundane into glorious shows!

Vistas of the Immediate

Look around, adventure calls,
From kitchen spills to shopping malls.
Every moment hides a gem,
Like oddball socks, a true mayhem.

Hello, mailbox, what's your score?
Spam or treasure – who knows more?
Junk food wrappers on the floor,
Tell a story worth exploring more.

Calls from friends, a banter spree,
Text messages that make us glee.
In the small talks, greatness found,
Joyful noise that spins around.

With open eyes, we'll seize the day,
Turning dull into a playful play.
Every tick of the clock is grand,
Grin wide, this moment's close at hand!

Echoes of a Hidden Journey

In search of gold at the rainbow's bend,
I tripped on a cloud, made a new friend.
He laughed at my quest for shiny delight,
And said, "Man, just make toast, it'll be alright!"

I wandered through fields of candy and cream,
But found that pure joy is a simple dream.
Forgotten my list of adventures grand,
Pursued a lost sock in the laundry land.

With a silly hat one day I did roam,
It danced in the breeze, called me its home.
We spun through the town, quite a silly pair,
Turns out, what I needed was fresh, funky air.

So next time you search for treasures untold,
Look right under your nose, it's worth more than gold.
For laughter's a gem, in the absurdity found,
In the echoes of life, joy knows no bound.

Moments of Magic

I laughed at my coffee, it winked from the cup,
I said, "You sly bard, will you perk me right up?"
It swirled in a dance, added foam with a flair,
"Just sip," it insisted, "You'll float like a chair!"

A cat on a skateboard dashed right through the park,
While a squirrel in a top hat hit a note on a lark.
This circus of moments I snagged with my net,
Left me giggling as I chased a sunset.

A puddle reflected my wild, woeful face,
As I jumped in with style, what a glorious place!
With each splash that I took, I was suddenly free,
Magic lives in mischief, oh why can't we see?

I'll keep my eyes open for joy's little quirks,
In this silly old world, it just happily works.
Who knew that in moments so perfectly small,
Lie the crackles of laughter that tickle us all?

Whispers of the Present

A gnome in my garden is planning a feast,
He's baking a cake with a few bits of yeast.
"Get off your phone!" he shouts up the tree,
"The sun is now shining, here's some cake for thee!"

Hopping through puddles, I sing with delight,
As raindrops are waltzing in shimmering light.
"Today is a gift!" chirps a bird from the eaves,
With feathers of laughter and joy that it weaves.

Around every corner, a giggle awaits,
In moments so simple, like playing with plates.
I juggled some fruits, took a tumble and fell,
But laughter erupted, and all was quite swell.

Let's toast to the now, with cupcakes and cheer,
For whispers of present spark joy, it is clear.
In the hustle of life, look around and embrace,
The wonder in mischief and each silly space.

Joys in the Everyday

The sun peeked in, with a smile on its face,
I tiptoed on toast crumbs, oh what a wild chase!
Toast danced with butter and sings through the air,
Life's little giggles hiding everywhere!

A sock puppet show put on by my cat,
With a dramatic flair, it wore my old hat.
Meowing the lines to a script made of dreams,
In the comedy chaos, pure joy brightly beams.

We hugged all the laundry, it clung like a friend,
Every shirt had a story, a laugh round the bend.
Dad's old joke book fell right on my toes,
Each pun I stumbled on tickled my nose.

So here's to the moments, both quirky and bright,
In the journey of life, let your heart take flight.
With giggles and gaffes, make every day sing,
For joys in the everyday are the real bling!

Home in the Present

In pajamas and fuzzy socks,
We laugh as time just mocks.
Coffee spills, oh what a sight,
But we're joyful, feeling light.

The cat jumps on the snack,
Chasing crumbs, what a knack!
We dance in the kitchen space,
With grace that has no trace.

Reality's a funny friend,
Bending rules, no need to pretend.
We trip over life's little cues,
In moments like these, we can't lose.

Home's in the chaos we weave,
In silly dances we believe.
Laughter echoes, what a show,
In this mess, life starts to glow.

A Tapestry of Choices

With options laid, like a buffet,
I choose cereal for dinner, hey!
Forget the gourmet, I'll be fine,
Just give me a bowl and some wine.

Each choice spins a funny yarn,
From socks that clash to breakfast barn.
Who knew that life could be this grand?
I'll take the silly over the planned.

Tangled paths that make me grin,
Like wearing socks where they don't fit in.
Life's choices could confuse a knight,
But I'm here laughing, feeling bright.

Adventure's folly is the game,
Making memories, not acclaim.
So bring it on, I'll take a spin,
With choices that make me laugh within.

Your Unwritten Story

Pages waiting, blank and bare,
Not a single word to share.
But give me a pen, let's take a chance,
And scribble down our wildest dance!

Every chapter, a twist or joke,
Like clumsy quips from the town folk.
With heroes who trip and fall,
Our tales are goofy, not grand at all.

Plot holes bigger than a shark,
But who needs sense? We've got a spark!
In doodles of friends, and epic blunders,
We find the fun beneath the wonders.

Write it messy, let it show,
In silly scenes, let laughter flow.
Your story's wonky; that's the key,
To finding joy in just being free.

In the Depths of Simplicity

In quiet moments, laughter grows,
From simple things, like garden hoes.
We plant a seed, then watch it sprout,
Oops! A weed – that's what life's about!

A cup of tea, a whispered joke,
Sometimes we fall for things we poke.
In the mundane, there's bliss to find,
In giggles shared, hearts unwind.

Let's cherish the soap suds that fly,
While washing dishes, who needs to sigh?
In the depths of daily grind,
A treasure chest of fun, we find!

So here's to life, so crisp and clear,
In every joke, we'll hold it dear.
In simple times, our hearts take wing,
Knowing laughter's the best bling.

The Beauty That Surrounds You

The cat in the window, it stares quite profound,
As if it knows secrets of all that abound.
A plant on the shelf, with leaves it will sway,
Whispering jokes in its own leafy way.

The sunbeam would dance on the coffee cup rim,
While I try to balance, oh where have I been?
The toast pops up singing, a musical cheer,
Life's little moments are perfectly clear.

A sock on the floor, a mystery unfolds,
It might be a portal to worlds yet untold.
With laughter and crumbs, I embrace the delight,
In simple things living, oh what a good sight!

So look all around, there's jest in the air,
Funny little happenings, treasures laid bare.
The chaos of socks and that dust bunny art,
Remind us to find joy and laugh with our heart.

Unseen Wonders Await

Beneath the couch lays a treasure untamed,
A lost Lego piece that's forever unnamed.
Spiders spin tales that make windows their stage,
As I clap for the drama, oh what a great age!

The fridge hums a tune of delightful surprise,
It grows fonder of leftovers, or so it implies.
The milk must be dancing, the cheese has a twirl,
In this grand kitchen show, my heart starts to whirl!

Outside my own door, a parade of the ants,
With tiny little hats, oh how they advance!
Each grain of their food is a hefty high score,
While I sit and watch them, I couldn't want more.

So peek through your window and look all around,
Life's rich tapestry is gleefully found.
In everything tiny, there's humor to steal,
And wonders surprise us with each silly reel.

In the Blink of an Eye

A coffee cup waltzes as I rush on by,
It spills on my notes, oh my oh my!
The dog chases shadows, does flips in the sun,
In moments like these, oh isn't this fun?

The clock ticks so sly, with mischievous glee,
It knows all my plans, and holds them at sea.
A minute can feel like a giggle at play,
While I juggle worries that float and decay.

My shoes have opinions, they tease with each stride,
"Stay off the wet grass, don't slip, take a ride!"
As puddles invite me to dance like a fool,
I find in the splashes, I'm nobody's tool.

So blink, and you'll miss all the joyous parade,
The silly distractions that life has conveyed.
In every small moment, a comedy thrives,
Just laugh at the chaos, it's here that we dive!

Fragments of Radiance

In corners of rooms, where sunlight does creep,
The dust motes are twirling, in whispers they leap.
A cat with a plush toy is plotting a scheme,
As it strokes my leg, 'tis now quite the team!

The toaster is moody, it only sings toast,
Yet crumpets and bagels it cares for the most.
While shadows are dancing, the curtains partake,
In this playful ballet, it's all about take!

The clock has a tickle, it laughs in delight,
Each hour brings shenanigans fresh from the night.
A squirrel with ambitions, it's acrobat trained,
On branches with swagger, oh what has it gained?

So gather these fragments, let laughter ignite,
In mundane adventures, find joy in the light.
Life's a fun riddle, just follow the clues,
And with all your heart, you can't help but choose!

Heartstrings of Connection

In a world of screens and likes,
We send our best wishes in bytes.
But here's the secret, hold your phone tight,
Laughter's the signal that shoots through the night.

Let's meet for coffee, it's on me,
We'll sip and spill our gossip spree.
Who cares about how many friends we might lack?
A good old chat keeps our hearts on track!

A meme, a wink, a dance out of tune,
Our quirks make the night feel like a festoon.
So put down your gadgets, take off the mask,
True joy is in asking the simplest of tasks!

Trust me, virtual can't beat the real,
Popcorn in hand, let's share what we feel.
Together we'll find the snacks we forgot,
Connection's the treasure that can't be bought!

An Invitation to Now

Why chase tomorrow, it's out of sight?
Let's put down the maps, and make today bright.
With socks that don't match and hair in a whirl,
We'll conquer our problems in a twirl!

Carrying worries like bags full of bricks,
We trip on our thoughts, doing acrobat tricks.
But what if we stopped and took a good look?
The present's a treasure, not just a book!

On Tuesdays we'll dance like the stars in the morn,
Each belly laugh louder, nobody's forlorn.
In mismatched pajamas, we'll host a grand ball,
Life's greatest wonders are seen when we stall!

So join this wild ride, no tickets required,
With spontaneity, everyone's inspired.
Let's play hopscotch on dreams that we found,
In each goofy moment, our joy will abound!

Finding Beauty in Routine

Wake up each morning, the alarm goes off,
Coffee in hand, give the world a scoff.
Check the fridge for breakfast's delight,
Last night's pizza? Oh, what a sight!

The commute's a dance to a tune that's my own,
Bopping in traffic, I'm never alone.
The routine's a circus, don't take it for granted,
Balloons full of humor cannot quite be slanted!

Lunch breaks are sneaky, a pizza surprise,
Caught with a fork, oh what a disguise!
On repeat with tasks, but watch how we play,
In mundane moments, we find our ballet!

Home with the fam, in PJs, we crash,
Spilling the tea over pizza and mash.
So here's to the rhythm that grooves us to cheer,
Finding the sparkle in each routine year!

Joys in the Simple

Slice of pie in the afternoon sun,
With crumbs on my face, hey, is this fun?
A stroll with the dog, both mutts in a race,
Chasing each squirrel with no hint of grace!

Flip-flops flapping, let's hear them clap,
Picnic in the park, who needs a map?
A game of tag with kids on the green,
Our shouts like thunder, a glorious scene!

With bubble gum bubbles and popsicle dreams,
We laugh till it hurts, or so it seems.
Life's little moments, like candy they sweet,
Our simple adventures, can't be beat!

So grab a spoon, let's dig into life,
Forget all the chaos and mundane strife.
In the simplest joys, our hearts learn to fly,
Embracing the silly 'neath this wide-open sky!

Seeds of Happiness

In the garden where joy blooms,
We dig for laughs, and not just looms.
Sprinkle smiles like seeds on the ground,
Watch the giggles grow all around.

Dancing tomatoes, singing peas,
Kale that's ticklish, oh what a tease!
Plant your worries in a pot,
Water with laughter, give it a shot.

Sunshine clouds with chocolate shade,
Silly squirrels in a serenade.
A patch of fun, a plot of cheer,
Harvest hilarity, year after year.

So grab a spade, let's have a riot,
In this quirky, joyful quiet.
The happy seeds we sow today,
Will grow into fun, come what may.

The Light in Your Hands

A candle flickers with a friendly grin,
Bouncing shadows dance on the ceiling, akin.
Grab a flashlight, brandish it bright,
What a show! It's party tonight!

Socks lit up like disco balls,
Flashy footwear that breaks the walls.
Wear your heart, or maybe your shoe,
Step into joy, let the fun ensue!

Glowing glow-sticks, let's find our groove,
Caution: too much glee may bust the move!
Raise a toast with lemonade in hand,
Cheers to being a silly band!

Bask in the glow of ridiculous dreams,
Follow the laughter, or so it seems.
Light-hearted antics, shine all day,
With smiles that chase the gloom away.

Gifts of the Mundane

A spoon that sings while stirring stew,
An old sock puppet, who'd guess it's you?
Mundane treasures in every nook,
Find the laughs in every hook.

The fridge hums a merry tune,
Leftover pizza talks to the moon.
Dirt on your shoes? A badge of glory,
Every mess has a funny story!

Tune into traffic, what a strange beat,
Horns playing tunes that can't be discreet.
Bump into life, like a dance with grace,
Just the way your cereal falls from space!

Even the chores can spark delight,
Waltzing with the broom feels just right.
Embrace the odd, let go the plain,
In the mundane lies the treasure train!

Close to You

A pet that howls at the break of dawn,
A partner that dances, their shoes all wrong.
Laughter echoes in the cozy room,
With silly faces that chase the gloom.

Cuddly pillows that want to chat,
A blanket fort where a friendship's at.
Snuggles wrapped in a joyful hug,
Sometimes warmth comes from a little bug!

The coffee pot keeps pouring cheer,
While toast pops up with a funny sneer.
Sharing bites, with crumbs all around,
In the chaos, happiness is found.

So stay close, let's slapstick away,
In our little world, we laugh and sway.
Here's to the funny, the joy anew,
All the magic lives, snuggled close to you!

The Secret in the Stillness

In silence, squirrels stash their nuts,
While pigeons argue over crumbs from cuts.
A breeze whispers secrets in the trees,
But I'm just searching for my lost keys.

The grass tickles toes that wiggle free,
As I contemplate life's big mystery.
Do ducks really know their quacking game?
Or are they just quacking for the fame?

Beneath the shade, a rogue ant parade,
Marching like they're in a grand charade.
If only I could join their jolly crew,
I'd finally conquer my morning stew.

But here I sit, a human afoul,
Thinking too hard, while they all scowl.
Maybe stillness isn't all that bad,
Just look at those ants, they seem so glad.

Here and Now

I'm here scratching my head, what to do?
While ice cream melts, and my cat sneezes too.
The clock ticks on, mocking my delay,
As I try to recall life's buffet.

Friends laugh loudly, with crumbs on their face,
While I trip over my shoelace in haste.
They say live today like it's all a game,
But I still fumble, isn't that just lame?

Birds dive in for bites of midair pie,
While I ponder about this old TV guy.
"Why's it always so funny?" I muse aloud,
Yet my own jokes barely please the crowd.

A moment unfolds, like a gift all its own,
With laughter and sprinkle-covered ice cream cone.
So here I am, taking it slow,
Today's a comedy show, don't you know?

Beyond the Horizon

Looking out past the hills and the trees,
Wondering if the sun has cranked up its fees.
What lies ahead? A treasure of sorts?
Or just more traffic on the way to the courts?

A pirate ship sails with a deck full of gold,
While I search for my other sock, so bold.
I imagine horizons filled with surprise,
While reality just rolls its weary eyes.

Oh! To be free like a kite in the sky,
Instead, I'm tethered to my couch nearby.
The horizon's great, full of possibilities wide,
But snacks are my compass, I just can't hide.

So here I'll stay, with my snacks and my dreams,
Beyond the horizon are louder screams.
Yet I'll keep gazing, with laughter's embrace,
Finding joy on this couch, my happy place.

The Gift of Today

Today is a present, wrapped in bright bows,
Worn out from dancing with its wrinkled clothes.
The coffee's cold, but my hopes stay warm,
As I look for life's next charming charm.

A dog sprawls across the neighbor's lawn,
While I step around puddles, yawning at dawn.
The mailman's whistling a ridiculous tune,
While I count my steps to the light of the moon.

Laughter erupts from the yard with a splash,
Kids in mud puddles, a glorious crash.
I envy their freedom, the joy of the day,
While my grown-up tasks seem to fumble and sway.

So here in this moment, I choose to be me,
With laughter and chaos, I'm happy and free.
The gift of today is both funny and bright,
I thank all the puddles for pure delight!

Whispers of the Present

In a world of to-do lists, we scramble around,
Searching for answers that never are found.
But the joy often hides in the silliest things,
Like a cat in a box, oh what joy it brings!

We race past the sunset, our hair in a flurry,
Chasing the next big thing, oh what a hurry!
Meanwhile, the laughter from kids at the park,
Is louder than deadlines, oh dear, what a lark!

A missed train, a wrong turn, we make it an art,
Every oops is a giggle, a brand new start.
Life's little hiccups, our quirky delight,
Dance like no one sees you, oh what a sight!

So embrace the odd moments, the blunders, the cheer,
For in between chaos, true magic is near.
With mismatched socks on and a grin ear to ear,
The best part of life is... simply being here!

Chasing Shadows at Noon

Stumbling through shadows, what's this I see?
A potato rolling past, quite carefree!
A flock of lost socks on a bicycle ride,
Each twist and each turn holds laughter inside!

Sunlight winks cheekily, bright in the sky,
While birds throw a party; oh my, oh my!
With ice cream for breakfast and cake at six,
We jump over puddles, oh what silly tricks!

The clock ticks away, but who keeps the score?
With dance moves that rival a clumsy dinosaur.
We chase down the giggles, let worries take flight,
For shadows at noon bring a joy so bright!

So let's skip through the chaos and sing silly tunes,
Life's far more delightful with sock-wearing goons.
Let's paint our existence in colors so bold,
Chasing shadows of laughter, never growing old!

Treasure in Everyday Glimpses

Oh, treasure isn't gold or a diamond so rare,
It's finding a coffee shop with plush, comfy chairs.
Where idleness whispers and laughs fill the air,
And baristas have quirks like a three-legged bear!

In simple bread crumbles and crumbs on the floor,
Lies the secret to smiles, and perhaps even more.
Like the cat on the windowsill, snoozing away,
In each glimpse of the mundane, joy decides to play.

The neighbor's loud sneezes might rattle your plans,
But maybe it sparks some impromptu dance spans.
With balloons from the market that swirl in the breeze,
Life's filled with treasure; just help yourself, please!

So cherish the moments; they glimmer like stars,
In a messy world peppered with doughnut-shaped cars.
Follow the giggles; let spontaneity lead,
For hidden in laughter, we find all we need!

Moments Wrapped in Time

Tick-tock, so the clock goes; what's a minute or two?
It's sipping on lemonade, just me and the view.
While ants hold a meeting, conspiring for crumbs,
It's refreshing to pause, enjoy, laugh, and hum!

We juggle our schedules, just like clowning pros,
But watch as the dog steals a sock, and it shows!
In the hustle of chores, let's find some delight,
A paper airplane flies with an amusing flight!

Moments wrapped tightly in laughter and cheer,
Bring ribbons of joy, though they may disappear.
In each sticky note scribbled with hopes,
We find the real magic in life's funny scopes.

So grab your umbrella if it looks like it'll rain,
Dance like a dork; ignore judgment in vain!
For life has its quirks; let's embrace every chime,
Moments are treasures, and they're yours, wrapped in time!

Glimmers in the Grit

In muddy shoes, I found a dance,
With every slip, I took a chance.
The world's a stage, and I'm the clown,
In the puddles, I wear my crown.

A pigeon coos as I take a spin,
He struts around like he's my kin.
I trip on laughter, roll in glee,
Life's a mess, but look at me!

The sun peeks through with a cheeky grin,
While I juggle coffee and a muffin tin.
The chaos sparkles, it's quite a show,
In the grit, we find our glow.

So here's to slips and silly falls,
Where joy erupts, and giggle calls.
In every stumble, there's gold to see,
Let's dance through the mess, you and me!

Gifts in the Gloam

Amidst the fog, I found my hat,
A rubber chicken, imagine that!
I walk with flair, like a grand parade,
In shadowy hues, my antics invade.

The twilight twinkles with little quirks,
Squirrels join me, busy with their perks.
A ninja cat does its shadow dance,
While I trip over my own romance.

Here's a fortune cookie on the street,
Telling me life's bizarre but sweet.
In the gloam, we sip on dreams,
Unraveling laughter, bursting seams.

So let's toast to the bizarre and quite absurd,
For in every corner, weirdness stirred.
With chuckles and snorts, the night unfolds,
In this crazy world, joy never grows old.

Simplicity's Soft Call

With just a sock and a leftover shoe,
I made a puppet, it's now my crew.
We chat and giggle, oh what a sight,
In simple joys, we find our light.

A paper boat floats down the drain,
It's on a mission and feeling no pain.
We sail through memories, so carefree,
Oh, life's magic, come play with me!

A squeaky toy and a slice of pie,
We concoct dreams as the hours fly by.
In little things, we find our role,
Simplicity whispers, filling the soul.

So here's a toast with fizzy cheer,
To laughter shared and a wink sincere.
In the mundane, all treasures lie,
Let's relish the calm, you and I!

Dawn in the Details

The coffee brews, it kicks and hops,
I spill it once while doing flips and flops.
A cat on my head, what a wild style,
I embrace the morning with a goofy smile.

Butterflies dance on the cereal flakes,
While my toast pops up, make no mistakes.
A juggling act with fruit and spree,
The day awakens with laughter's decree.

In mismatched socks and a crooked tie,
I strut like a king, oh me, oh my!
The sunlight sparkles on jammy bread,
In every detail, joy's widespread.

So let's step into this bright ballet,
With giggles and quirks in the grand array.
In the dawn's glow, let's take our stance,
For every moment, we shall prance!

This Place, This Time

In a room full of socks, where mismatches reside,
We dance with our worries, let the chaos slide.
The ceiling's a canvas, the floor's a dance hall,
Our laughter ignites, we're having a ball.

With a fridge full of nothing, we feast like kings,
On leftovers and ketchup, oh what joy it brings.
The cat's our applause, he jumps with delight,
This right here, this moment, feels perfectly tight.

The Secret Door to Contentment

Behind the squeaky fridge, there's a door snug and tight,
Where chicken nuggets whisper tales of delight.
In a realm of confetti, and joy in each bite,
We sip on our soda, and everything's right.

Here's to laundry baskets that double as thrones,
To conversations with plants, and dodging the phones.
The pets are our audience, they cheer and they play,
In this secret utopia, we'll frolic each day.

Unraveled Possibilities

With mismatched shoes, we take on the street,
Our paths, like rubber bands, twist and repeat.
We stumble on purpose, embrace each odd view,
In the parade of the goofy, we find what is true.

From pancake portraits to cereal lore,
We paint our daydreams on big kitchen floors.
In the land of the lost keys, we flourish and glow,
Each moment's a gem, let the laughter flow.

A Step into the Now

At a table of crumbs, where stories collide,
The coffee is cold, but we raise it with pride.
With socks on our hands, we craft our own fun,
In this messy old chaos, we bask in the sun.

Each tick of the clock brings a giggle or two,
The remote's our throne, and we wave it like a cue.
Life shrinks to a giggle, with friends all around,
In this glorious moment, happiness is found.

Here Lies Abundance

In a world where cake is free,
And ice cream flows like a sea,
The treasure's not in distant lands,
It's underfoot—just look, it stands.

Why chase the gold when spoons are bright,
Under the couch, there's a dim light,
A snack or two might just appear,
First, check your pockets—hold them near.

With every drop that falls from skies,
Jokes and laughter are no surprise,
The riches found in silly toys,
Make golden days from mundane noise.

So here's to crumbs and pizza bites,
The joy in finding missing tights,
In abundance laugh, don't always seek,
For life's a party—tickle your cheek.

The Gifts Within Reach

A sock put on the wrong foot, hey,
Could lead to laughter in the fray,
Not every prize hangs on a shelf,
Sometimes it's fun just being oneself.

A cozy chair, a junk food stash,
That secret spot where cookies crash,
The gifts we seek are near, it's true,
Mostly they hide, just peek askew.

Each silly meme steals time away,
A dance-off here will save the day,
Grab your friends, and make a mess,
The spark of joy is pure finesse.

So look around, don't pull your hair,
In every game, there's love to share,
The gifts are close, don't lose your cheer,
In every chuckle, draw them near.

In the Dance of Moments

A jelly bean won't change the world,
But it sure makes your taste buds swirl,
Each funny dance you start to sway,
Can turn a gray dull into play.

Grab your hat and spin around,
A penguin's waddle is quite profound,
The clock may tick, but hearts take flight,
In every giggle, life feels right.

Moments passed can't be retraced,
Yet in the laughter, time is faced,
So shimmy close, and take that chance,
For joy is in a silly dance.

With every joke and playful jest,
Forget the worry, feel the zest,
In this bright twist of every turn,
The dance of moments—oh, how we yearn.

The Wonder of Being Here

In a world of socks that disappear,
Who knew that laughter thrives so near?
A squirrel steals seeds right off your porch,
Hilarity blooms like a torch.

Why fret for dreams that float away,
When sunbeams shine on a dull day?
Balloons can pop, but spirits soar,
Here's to the fun—the endless door.

Among the chaos, let's not forget,
The joy in friendship that you beget,
So raise a toast with lemonade,
To all the mess and plans delayed.

In the wonder of the silly now,
Embrace the strange, no need to bow,
Gifts come wrapped, in oddest ways,
So laugh it off, and bask in rays.

Dancing with the Unknown

Twirl with socks on the floor,
Spin and laugh, who keeps score?
The fridge light flickers bright,
Chasing snacks deep into the night.

A dance partner who's a chair,
Wiggle, jiggle, don't you stare!
The cat joins in with a pounce,
Two left feet, but we still bounce.

Every step, a crazy flop,
Tangled limbs, but we don't stop.
Salsa or tango, who's to say?
As long as smiles lead the way!

So here we boogie, full of cheer,
With every misstep, my dear.
Dancing through this twisty ride,
Let's follow whimsy, and not hide!

In the Midst of It All

Juggling laundry piles so high,
Missed the phone call, oh my, oh my!
Coffee spills, and so do dreams,
While my breakfast loudly screams.

Chasing kids, or maybe a cat,
Every moment's a game of that!
Wheels squeak and the dog runs free,
Trying to catch what's chasing me.

Dinner prep? A thirty-second thrill!
Stirring fast with endless will.
The oven's timer goes off like a horn,
Taco Tuesday? I'm not even worn!

In the chaos, there's a funny spark,
Finding joy in the wildest park.
Life's a mess, a colorful ball,
And I'm dancing through it all!

Searching No More

Keys lost under the couch again,
Phantom socks, where have you been?
I thought I'd find my missing shoe,
But here's a spoon; oh, who knew?

Maps and lists clutter my mind,
Turns out, I was just blind!
The fridge is where snacks reside,
Check there first, with pride.

No need to climb a mountain high,
For ice cream awaits nearby.
In a world of endless quest,
The best delays bring out the zest.

No more Googling, I confess,
To find joy in this sweet mess.
Lost and found; it's all the same,
In quirks and giggles, we stake our claim.

What Lies Under the Surface

The carpet hides treasures galore,
Dust bunnies? Wait, I found four!
A sandwich from yesteryear creeps,
In this wild hunt, humor leaps.

Underneath piles of unfolded clothes,
An ancient T-shirt, nobody knows.
Old sneakers whisper stories long,
Each mute item sings its song.

Peeking under, I find a toy,
A little fish that used to bring joy.
Hidden gems in the mundane chase,
Who knew my home would hold such grace?

What lies beneath? Let's not fret,
In quirky finds, we won't forget.
Tripping over the past is grand,
Every stumble a treasure planned!

Finding Gold in the Soil

In a garden so messy, I dug with a smile,
Found a treasure of carrots, though it took quite a while,
Digging for riches, I struck gold with a cheer,
Turns out my fortune was just a root beer!

The weeds danced around like they owned the place,
But my shovel just chuckled, 'Let's pick up the pace!'
With dirt on my nose, I felt like a king,
Who knew that the soil could offer such bling?

Each toss of the earth brought laughter and cheer,
For every lost item, my garden's sincere,
Old boots and a spoon, a great mystery show,
I'll host a grand party for all of this 'gold'!

So here's to the mess, the laughter, the fun,
In my soil, I treasure, not just what I've won,
For the joy in the digging is worth more than gold,
And I'll keep on gardening till I'm gray and old!

A Symphony of Now

Close your eyes tight, feel the tickle of air,
The song of the moment, a sweet little snare,
Hear the burp of a bird, whistle of a breeze,
This orchestra's playing with mischievous ease!

Chasing after whispers of yesterday's dreams,
I tripped over laughter, so bursting at seams,
Dancing with shadows that splashed in the sun,
Realized each heartbeat is simply pure fun!

With each tiny moment, a note we can strum,
The piano of life has a rhythm of gum,
Sticky and silly, it slows where it should,
Let's clap it together, it's all very good!

So let's make a ruckus, sing songs on the run,
For the symphony's waiting, so don't miss the fun,
In the hustle of now, find a jingle or two,
Life's best improvisations are made just by you!

The Color of Contentment

Woke up one morning, my socks weren't a pair,
But I smiled and I laughed, what a colorful wear,
In mismatched patterns, I strutted so proud,
Like a peacock in traffic, I sang to the crowd!

Coffee spilled over, the cat chased a mouse,
Each incident painted a scene in my house,
Splashes of chaos, a canvas so bright,
Ah, the colors of life make everything right!

With each little blunder, I simply would grin,
For joy's in the journey, not needing to win,
Life's palette is wild, with a funny hue,
I'll paint on the canvas, with laughter anew!

So let's swish our paints, with a dash and a swirl,
In the gallery of crazy, watch my colors twirl,
For happiness lives in the shades that we choose,
With a wink and a smile, how can we lose?

Realms of Reflection

Peeking in mirrors, with a grin on my face,
I see silly versions, not bound by space,
In funhouse dimensions, I twirl and I bend,
Finding joy in the wobbles, on me I depend!

Reflections are laughter, they dance with delight,
Silly shadows in hallways, let's join in the fight,
Against frowns and the sighs, we'll brighten the mood,
With a quip and a quirk, we'll make it a brood!

Each twist holds a treasure, each giggle a gem,
Like clouds in a storm, let's not seize 'em, condemn,
We'll bounce off the walls, with a clatter and cheer,
In realms of reflection, we'll feast on the sheer!

So here's to the fun of the mountains we climb,
In mirrors we find the most laughter-filled rhyme,
For life is the quest, filled with all sorts of quirks,
And in every reflection, the humor just lurks!